Guided Meditations
Volume 3

How to Teach Youth
to Pray
Using Scripture

Jane Reehorst, B.V.M.

BROWN-ROA
A Division of Harcourt Brace & Company

Dubuque, Iowa

ISBN 0–697–17596–0

22 23 24 25 015098 13 12 11 10

Manufactured by Edwards Brothers, Lillington, NC, United States of America,
March 2010, 801440 / 22nd.

Acknowledgements

I would like to thank my brother John and his wife Carole, my niece and nephew, Susan and Michael, my brother Dick and his wife Eileen, and friends who supported and encouraged me while I was writing this book. Of all the young people who gave time and input helping me to address the needs and questions of their age group, I would especially like to mention Louie Mansilla, Iliana Fuentes, Sieria Licon, Ivan Guzman, and Maribel Morales.

Table of Contents

Why Does God Let This Happen?

Who Am I?

Journey of Faith

Foreword:
Teaching Youth to
Pray Using Scripture

This is a simple but powerful book on teaching young people *how* to pray—using active imagination. It is written specifically for young people in junior and senior high. In speaking to and interviewing young people from all walks of life, I discovered a common thread of concerns and questions. The subjects of the meditations in this book attempt to address some of these concerns and questions.

The goal of this book is to help the catechist lead the class into a Gospel scene and meet Jesus personally, affecting not only their present prayer life but building a foundation for their adult prayer life. This approach to prayer has been in the Church for centuries.

It is important that the teacher participate in the meditation as it is being presented. In order to do this effectively, it is suggested that, prior to the presentation, the teacher spend some time meditating on the Gospel to be presented, becoming comfortable with this prayer form. This also allows for the opportunity of tailoring the meditation to meet the needs of the class. The process for meditation is outlined in detail. Read slowly, with a slight pause where indicated (. . .).

A Change in Format for Retreats

As day or week—end retreats are often given for this age group, there has been a change in format in this book. Along with the individual meditations there are also grouped meditations under various subject matters. For example, one group of meditations addresses the question, "Why Does God Allow This to Happen?" The class is led into three separate meditations addressing the hardship and suffering of Mary, then Joseph, and then Jesus. Since each meditation has its own follow-up, the catechist has the choice of using an individual meditation or all three, depending on time and situation (classroom or retreat).

Spontaneous Prayer

This may not happen until a spirit of trust is built up within the class. However, the catechist is encouraged to give an example of praying spontaneously. (A suggestion of prayer follows each meditation.) Invite the class to offer their prayers, wait for a minute, and then gently lead them out of the Gospel scene.

Quiet Time

Allow 1—2 minutes. Watch for a restlessness in the class for your guide. A minute is a long time for a young person.

Journal Writing

The purpose of this activity is to teach young people to listen to the Spirit within. It is a simple and spontaneous activity and needs little explanation. After the young people write down any thoughts they might have had during the meditation, it would be a good idea to note the date and Scripture passage. A special loose-leaf note book for each person could be used for journal writing.

Discussion

Sharing their reflections teaches young people to listen to God's Spirit speaking through others. *Small groups* are less threatening in sharing. Someone in each small group could be designated to take notes to share in the large group sharing.

Para-Liturgy

The para-liturgy is an experience of the community coming together before God, and placing their faith in Jesus who shows us the Father. Active participation and sharing are most important.

Activities

The activities give opportunities to young people to learn to go forth and share the Good News with others.

These suggestions are made with the thought in mind that the teacher will add to, subtract from, or change the suggestions if and when opportunities present themselves. There is only one rule: ''Keep it simple.''

A Place to Meet Jesus

By the Sea of Galilee

Teacher Introduction

This is a special meditation, one that is very important in building a relationship with Jesus. We will be creating a place in our imagination where we can go any time we wish and be alone with Jesus. It is a way to become quiet within, to listen and, in this silence, to be aware of the presence of God. This is a place where you can come quietly and be surrounded by the healing power of God, not complicating things by filling your time with conversation if you do not wish to, but to allow the healing power of God to surround and heal you.

The place we are going to is by the Sea of Galilee. The town of Capernaum is located there. The people of Capernaum welcomed Jesus, and believed in him. This town became the home base for Jesus and his disciples. Jesus felt comfortable here. What better place is there to be than by the Sea of Galilee where Jesus often walked!

1

Meditation

(Teachers: A good background for this meditation is the cassette tape *Sounds of the Ocean.*)

Close your eyes. . . . Take a deep breath . . . and relax. . . . You are standing by the sea. . . . Begin to walk down the shore . . . the very same shore where Jesus walked . . . where he preached . . . where he came to be alone with the Father. Feel the sacredness of this place. . . . Walk closer to the water's edge and allow the sea to wash over your feet. . . . The water is cool, isn't it? . . . Just stand here, allowing the coolness of the sea to wash over your feet. . . . Relax. . . . Enjoy. . . . It's a beautiful time to be here, for the sun is slowly setting, painting the sky and sea an orange gold. Watch the sun go down. . . . Feel the cool wet sand under your feet. . . . Jesus must have done the very same thing you are doing. . . . He must have watched the beauty of the sunset, keenly aware of nature. . . . Look down the beach. . . . Sea gulls are silently nestled in the sand facing the sun. . . . Only a few of them circle the water, calling out to each other. . . . Take a deep breath and let the freshness of this sea air fill your lungs. . . .

Look for a place where you would like to sit. . . . There are some rocks down the shore a bit . . . the ones reaching into the sea. . . . In back of you, there are more rocks away from the water, dug into the warm sand. . . . Or you can sit on the sand . . . choose a place where you feel comfortable. . . .

2

(Pause and give students time to select their special place.) This is your place. . . . Be still. . . . Enjoy the sounds of the sea . . . the sky that seems a deeper orange and gold as the sun silently sinks into the sea. . . .

As you sit here, be aware of the presence of someone who has quietly sat down beside you. . . . Feel your heart beat faster and a joy seeping through you. . . . You know without looking that the one who is with you is Jesus, a very special friend of yours. . . . Jesus does not speak. . . . He doesn't have to . . . for he knows he is welcome to be here with you, his friend. . . . Try not to speak. . . . Enjoy this moment together . . . in peace and quiet . . . in harmony . . . no need for words. . . . Just be.

(Teacher: If you wish, you can say, ''I will leave you alone to spend a few minutes with Jesus.'' However, you do not have to do it with this meditation.)

Prayer

Jesus, it is good to be here with you, relaxing with you, not having to say anything, just knowing that I am accepted for who I am, and loved by you. Thank you for being here with me. I'm glad I have a special place to meet you, even for a minute during the day. So often before, I wanted to talk to you but didn't know where to go. Now we have a place together, just you and I. Amen. (Invite spontaneous prayer.)

It is time to leave. Quietly get up and begin to walk away, knowing that you can come back here any time and Jesus will be waiting. Open your eyes, and come back into the room.

Journal Writing

Write down any thoughts you might have had during this meditation. As this was a quiet meditation with no need for talking, express any feelings you had during or after the meditation.

Sharing

In small groups, discuss the feelings the students had during or after the meditation and how they feel about having a place to go to talk over problems with Jesus, to listen, and to be quiet.

Activity

To help their place become more vivid to them have the class either draw, paint, or make a collage of what they pictured in their imagination. Suggest that they put the picture on a wall in their room. Play soft music in the background.

Suggested Music: *Taizé* (GIA Publications)

True Fear

Luke 12:1–6; Luke 22:39–45; Mark 14:32–42

Teacher Introduction

Today we are going to approach the subject of fear and, after we share our thoughts about fear, we will turn to Jesus' teaching and example about fear. First of all, what is your definition of fear? Is fear bad? Does it have a place in our life? What are some of our fears, either real or imaginary? We'll list them on the board and see if we have any fears in common. (Give time to discuss the common fears.) Can you give examples of people who let fear run their lives? Can you give examples of people doing something in spite of their fear? Was there a time in Jesus' life when he went on in spite of his fear?

In order to deal with our fears and place them in a proper perspective in our lives, we are first going to be with Jesus when he teaches about fear. Then we will go to the Mount of Olives and see how Jesus dealt with fear.

5

First Meditation—*Fearing God,* Luke 12:1–6

Close your eyes. . . . Take a deep breath . . . and relax. . . . Let's be with Jesus and his disciples as he preaches to a large crowd outside one of the small towns in Judea. . . . You and the disciples are seated close to Jesus on a little hill that is just high enough to allow the people gathered to see and hear Jesus. . . . Try to enter into the scene. . . . Be aware of the warm day . . . the grass that acts as a cushion for you. . . . Enjoy the freshness of the air. . . . It's good to be with Jesus, isn't it, even though his message today has been strong, even harsh at times? . . . Experience your faith in Jesus . . . your trust that what he is saying is out of love for you. . . . But then listen to the reaction of the crowd . . . the muttering of the people gathered here today. . . . Study the faces around you. . . . Some people look anxious, don't they? . . . Other faces seem filled with hope. . . . Notice the man right in front of Jesus. . . . His face radiates happiness, doesn't it? . . . Contrast his face with faces of the Pharisees just behind him. . . . Observe their tight lips and judgmental expressions. . . . But wait, Jesus is raising his hand to silence the people. . . . Feel the heaviness of the silence that quickly sets in. . . . All eyes are on Jesus as he begins again to teach. . . . "I tell you, my friends," Jesus begins. . . . He pauses, his eyes searching the faces before him. "Do not be afraid of those who kill the body but cannot afterward do anything worse. I will show you whom to fear: fear God, who after killing has the authority to throw into hell. Believe me, He is the one you must fear." Jesus waits. . . . The people

6

seem divided, don't they? . . . Listen to the low muttering begin again. . . . Jesus turns to you. . . . His eyes search your face. . . . He places his hand on your arm. . . . Feel the touch of Jesus' hand on your arm. . . . What is Jesus trying to say to you? . . . Now he turns to the crowd and continues . . .

"Aren't five sparrows sold for two pennies? Yet not one sparrow is forgotten by God. . . . Even the hairs of your head have all been counted. . . . So do not be afraid, you are worth much more than many sparrows." . . . Jesus turns to you again . . . softly calls you by name to get your attention . . . and asks, "Do you understand what I have just said about God's love for you? . . . Are people supposed to fear those who love them? . . . Now tell me . . . why are you so often fearful? . . . Let me help you with these fears of yours." . . . Jesus waits for your response. . . .

I will give you a few minutes of silence to listen and speak to Jesus.

It is time to leave for we have to go somewhere else. As the people crowd around Jesus asking him questions, quietly get up and walk away, keeping his message to you deep within your heart.

Second Meditation — *Agony in the Garden,*
Luke 22:39–45; Mark 14:32–42

We are now going to be with Jesus in the Garden of Olives just outside of Jerusalem. . . . Close your eyes. Take a deep breath . . . and relax. . . . See before you a grove of olive trees. . . . This is the place where Jesus often comes to pray when he is in Jerusalem. . . . You are with Jesus and his apostles. . . . It is late. . . . You have just left the upper room where Jesus celebrated the Passover meal with you and his disciples. . . . Peter is walking next to you. . . . He bends his head toward you and whispers . . . "I wish we were far away from this place. . . . Jesus is in danger . . . I know it." The moon is so bright tonight that you can see the worried expression on Peter's face. . . . Feel your own heart begin to race. . . . Jesus in danger! . . . The olive trees seem to be standing guard over the garden, but they don't offer much comfort, do they? . . . No one is talking. . . . Everyone seems to be deep within his own thought. . . . This is not the kind of experience you are used to when you are with Jesus, is it? . . . So different . . . almost scary. . . . Your close friend could be arrested at any minute. . . . Then why does Jesus hang around here? Maybe you should go over and ask him. . . . Walk up to Jesus. . . . Walk close to him. . . . Can you feel his stress and anguish? . . . Before you can say anything, Jesus stops. . . . "Stay here," he tells all of you . . . but then he motions to Peter, James and John, and you to follow him. . . . The five of you walk further into the garden. . . . Jesus stops

8

again . . . looks sorrowfully at you . . . sighs and places his hand over his heart and almost moans his words, "The sorrow in my heart is so great that it almost crushes me." Jesus points to an olive tree, looks at his three disciples and says, "Stay here and keep watch." . . . Peter, James, and John look puzzled, but obey. They walk over to the tree and sit down. . . . Jesus looks at you . . . studies your face . . . and speaks one word, "Come." . . . Follow Jesus. . . . He walks up the path a short distance . . . stops . . . throws himself on the ground . . . and begins to pray. . . . Listen. . . . You can hear the words of Jesus' prayer, . . . "Father, all things are possible with you. . . . If you will . . . take this cup of suffering away from me." . . . Jesus sighs deeply . . . and is silent. Kneel close to Jesus. . . . Place your hand on his head to comfort him. . . . Feel the dampness of his hair . . . the shaking of his body . . . the fear . . . the pleading to escape the suffering he knows is about to befall him. . . . Listen. . . . Jesus is continuing to pray, . . . "Yet not what I want, but what you want." . . . Words spoken in this terrible fear. . . . "Yet not what I want, but what you want." . . . Stay with Jesus . . . in his fear . . . in his surrender to God's will. . . . I will leave you alone with Jesus.

Journal Writing

We are not going to leave Jesus just yet. Stay with him and listen. Then quietly write in your journal any thoughts and feelings you might have while you are here by him in the Garden.

9

Prayer

Jesus, it is time for me to leave you. Thank you for allowing me to be here and experience your fear with you. I never realized that you suffered fear like I do sometimes. Now I know you understand me, Jesus. Teach me to fear those who can lead me away from you, turning me away from your love and our friendship, and, Jesus, give me courage to face my fears and see them for what they are. I praise and thank you for this time with you. Amen. (Invite spontaneous prayer.)

Sharing

In small groups, tell the class to share the thoughts and feelings they had during these meditations. Let them choose a group recorder. Guide the class by asking if they had any changes in their thoughts about their attitude toward fear. If so, what brought about this change in thought? Try to be specific.

In the large group, the small—group recorders give input from their group. (Luke 12:4—6 may need to be clarified for the students.)

■ What did Jesus mean by saying that we should not be afraid of someone who can kill us, but rather fear God?

■ What worse experience can happen to us after we are killed?

10

■ On the one hand, Jesus is telling us to fear God because He can throw us into hell. Then, in verse 6, Jesus is telling us how much God loves us. Are these statements contradictory?

Activity

(Before this activity, have on hand helium balloons, one or two for each person.)

1. Individuals decide which fears (no more than two) they would like to be free of.

2. Create a symbol for each fear.

3. With a felt marker, draw this symbol on a balloon.

4. When class is finished, go outside and let each person send his or her fear balloon into the air. Make it a celebration!

Para-Liturgy

Prayer: Psalm 23:4—Even if I go through the deepest darkness, I will not be afraid, Lord, for you are with me. Your shepherd's rod and staff protect me. (Have a copy for each member of the class.)

Preparation: Set up a brazier (or grill) and coals. (If you use this powerful symbol, the class will experience their fear going up in smoke as an offering to the Father in Jesus' name and, thus, a release of their fear.)

Prepare an altar. Place on it the Bible, a candle, and other decorations. Decide on some symbol of God's love for us. A shepherd's staff with the name *Jesus*—or the *Chi Rho* on it—would follow through on Psalm 23. One symbol for each member of the class is placed on the altar.

Have each member of class write one fear on a slip of paper. Give each person words to the song *Be Not Afraid.*

Liturgy

■ Ask the class to gather around the altar.

■ To help the class return to a prayerful mood, invite the students to again go to the Garden of Olives. (Allow a few moments for this, until you sense a quietness.)

■ Read Psalm 23:1–3, then invite individual class members to *bring up* their fear symbol and place it on the altar (or burn it in the brazier). Recite Psalm 23:4 and pick up the symbol of God's love. When this is over, read Psalm 23:5–6. Conclude by singing *Be Not Afraid.*

Suggested Music: *Be Not Afraid* by Bob Dufford, S.J. (NALR); *Stay With Me* from Taizé (GIA Publications); *I Have Seen the Lord* by Ron Griffen (Leaven Productions).

Respecting the Dignity of Others

The Woman Caught in Adultery
John 8:4–11

Teacher Introduction

Have you ever been sorry for something you did or said to someone else when you were angry? Have you ever been so angry with someone that you would like to have harmed that person or you even wished that person were dead? When the passion of anger dominates you, are you able to reason things out? What do some people do when they are extremely angry? Follow their impulse to harm or kill? Are they justified in this? Are there alternatives? If so, what are they? Do we feed our anger by constantly thinking about the wrong done to us? Is this wise? Is there a time limit for calming down our anger?

The same can be applied to the passions that are aroused in our sexual drive. We can feed this drive, using another to satisfy ourselves, therefore harming the other person. Sometimes we follow our

13

impulses, excuse ourselves, and blame others. Explain whether the media helps or hinders our moral outlook on life.

This is a difficult subject. It is always challenging us. Even in Jesus' time, without the media, there were prostitutes. The one mentioned in the Gospels was "the woman caught in adultery." She sold her body for money. She was misused by the men in the town and, at the same time, was looked down upon by them for what she was. They judged her for being sinful but did not look at themselves, at their own sinful act! In Jesus' time, adultery was punishable by death; for women, this meant being stoned to death.

Meditation

Today, we are going to be with Jesus when he was asked to judge a woman caught in adultery. We need to learn from Jesus his attitude toward sin and us. Close your eyes. . . . Take a deep breath . . . and relax. . . . You are with Jesus and his disciples in the outer court of the Temple in Jerusalem. . . . Jesus is preaching here today. . . . Notice the large crowd gathered around him. . . . Most of them are eagerly listening to him . . . but, if you look at the outer edge of the crowd, you will see some frowns and sneers . . . nonbelievers and doubters. . . . It's the same story today, isn't it? . . . Walk over and sit next to Jesus. . . . Peter and John give you a welcome smile as they move over and let you sit by them, next to Jesus. . . . It's good to be here, isn't it? . . . Become aware of a peace filling you. . . . Listen to Jesus' voice . . . strong, yet kind . . . authority, yet love. . . . He gives you the feeling of being totally accepted, doesn't he? . . . No wonder these people like to be near him. . . . Look! . . . There is a disturbance at the crowd's edge. . . . Some men are pushing their way through . . . and pushing a woman ahead of them. . . . By their clothes, you can tell they are the Pharisees and the scribes. . . . Jesus stops speaking and watches. . . . Notice that everyone is watching them . . . and unconsciously making room for them to pass. . . . Look, that man pushes the woman so hard that she now falls at the feet of Jesus. . . . It's hard to see what she looks like because her hair is so long it covers her face . . . but listen to her sobbing. . . . It's frightening to watch someone being treated so harshly, isn't it? . . . Jesus now looks at the woman . . . then at her accusers . . . and silently waits for them to speak. . . . See that sneering Pharisee begin to step forward. . . . He scornfully draws his cloak around him so it won't touch the woman. . . . He points to her and says to Jesus, "Teacher, this woman was caught in the act of adultery. . . . In our Law, Moses commanded that such a woman be stoned to death. . . . Now what do you say?" . . . He steps back . . . folds his arms . . . stares at Jesus and waits. . . .

John nudges you and whispers, "They are trying to trap Jesus as usual." . . . Peter leans over and adds, "If Jesus says to punish her, his teachings on forgiveness become worthless. . . . If he doesn't say punish her, then they will say that he is against the Law of Moses." . . . John and Peter seem to

hold their breath as they turn and watch Jesus.
. . . Feel the heavy silence in this crowd. . . .
Everyone's eyes are on Jesus . . . silently waiting.
. . .

Jesus says nothing. . . . He just stoops down
and begins to write in the dirt with his finger. . . . He
stands . . . studies the faces of the accusers and
says, "Whichever one of you has committed no sin,
throw the first stone." . . . He stoops down and
continues to write in the dirt. . . . Look. . . . The
accusers are slowly leaving. . . . The woman looks
up . . . watches her accusers leave . . . turns to
Jesus, looking up into his face. . . . Jesus looks at
the woman. . . . "Where are they? Is there no one
left to condemn you?" he asks. . . . The woman
slowly shakes her head and says, "No one, sir."
. . . Notice her pleading eyes. . . . Jesus speaks
again, "I am not going to pass judgment on you,
either. Go . . ." She sighs . . . begins to get up off
the ground . . . but Jesus holds his hand up, stops
her and says, "But from now on, sin no more." . . .
Her second chance. . . .

It was a close call, wasn't it . . . this ugly
death by stoning? . . . You, the disciples, Jesus, and
the others watch the woman hurry away. . . . Jesus
sighs . . . turns to you . . . smiles . . . calls you by
name and walks over to you. . . . He places his arm
around your shoulders and looks into your eyes,
"Yes, she has a second chance . . . I will help her,
for my love and strength will always surround her."
. . . Jesus steps back . . . places his hands on your
shoulders and asks, "Tell me, what have you learned

here today that will help you in your own life?''
Jesus waits for you to respond. . . . I will give you a
silent time now to respond and listen.

Prayer

Jesus, I am thankful that you are a God of
love and forgiveness and not one waiting for me to
fall so that you can condemn me. I know that you
want me to tell of your love and forgiveness to those
who come into my life. Help and guide me, Jesus, as
opportunities present themselves to me. As you have
forgiven me so many times, giving me my second
chances, help me to forgive those who have hurt or
harmed me. Amen. (Invite spontaneous prayer.)

It is time to leave. Say good-bye to Jesus.
Turn and begin to walk away. Open your eyes and
come back into the room.

Journal Writing

Write down any thoughts or feelings you had
during your encounter with Jesus.

Sharing (small groups or class discussion)

1. Did you wonder about the innocence of those
   who accused the woman? What were your
   thoughts about the situation?

17

2.   Have you ever met people in your life like the scribes and Pharisees — condemning and unforgiving? How did you feel?

3.   About the "second chance" — do you think that the woman will have a struggle in changing her ways? Or, did she have it made since, after all, she met Jesus face to face?

4.   When will "second chances" end? Is there a limit to "second chances?"

5.   What do you think the purpose was in recording this incident in the life of Jesus?

Liturgy

A Penance Service — Theme: "A Second Chance"

Preparation: Besides the Bible and candle, have the crucifix in a predominant place. Prepare large nails or spikes by pasting on them the words, "Second Chance" (one for each person).

We all have our own personal struggles, our own crosses that we are nailed to, things we don't like about ourselves, things we know that are wrong or harmful to ourselves and others, yet we go ahead and do them anyway, disappointing ourselves. Right now, we are going to ask Jesus to help us think of one thing that jeopardizes our relationship with him. And, when we have thought of this, we will ask Jesus' help to change this one thing in our lives, this thing that nails us to our cross.

Quietly go to the outer court of the Temple once more. Jesus is there waiting. Sit quietly with him and listen. (Play a quiet song, like the *Taizé* tape.)

When the music is over, recite together parts of either Psalm 138 or 139.

Invite class members to place their nails of "Second Chance" on the altar at any time during the Psalm prayer. Close with a song.

Suggested Music: *Come to the Water* by John Foley, S.J. (NALR).

You Are Loved

The Last Supper
John 13–17

Teacher Introduction

Have you known someone who felt unloved? What does the term "conditional love" mean? Give examples of conditional love. Is it important to feel loved? Why? Give some examples of what it means to be loved. Who are the people in our lives that we expect to love us? What are some of the expectations we have of someone who loves us? We are told that God the Father loves us. Do we have proof of this? Do we doubt this?

All through his public life Jesus showed his love for people by his actions. He also told them of his Father's love for them. It was at the Last Supper, his final meal with his apostles, that Jesus spoke his final words of love for us. Even though he knew that within a few hours he would be arrested, tortured, ridiculed, and killed, he thought of us first—not of himself. To help us realize this we are going to be with Jesus and listen to his words to us.

Meditation

Close your eyes. . . . Take a deep breath . . . and relax . . . It is the day before the Passover Festival. Jesus knows that the hour has come for him to leave the world and go to the Father. He always loved those of us who are in the world and are his own and he loves us to the very end.

Let's go now to the upper room and sit next to Jesus at the table where he and his apostles have just finished the Passover meal. . . . Experience this upper room for a moment. . . . Look at the dancing shadows cast on the walls by the candles that light the room. . . . Smell the aroma of the lamb and wine and other foods that still permeate the room from the meal. . . . Study the faces of the apostles that are seated around the table. . . . Notice their serious expressions and their worried quick glances toward Jesus. . . . Hear their whispers to each other. . . . A woman quietly removes the remaining dishes from the table. . . . She glances quickly at Jesus . . . and hurries away. Jesus has been exceptionally quiet. . . . Maybe that is why the apostles seem worried. . . . But now he begins to speak. . . . The apostles become silent . . . lean forward . . . and listen. . . .

"My children," Jesus begins, "I shall not be with you very much longer. . . . I give you a new commandment: love one another." Jesus pauses . . . looks into your eyes . . . and places his hand on yours. . . . Feel the pressure of Jesus' hand . . . his warmth and strength coming toward you. . . . "As I have loved you, so you must love one another."

Peter breaks in, "Where are you going, Lord?" . . .
Jesus continues to hold your hand and says to all of
you, "Do not be worried and upset. Believe in God
and also in me. . . . I am going to prepare a place for
you. . . . I would not tell you this if it were not so.
. . . I will come back and take you to myself so that
you will be where I am." . . .

For a moment, study this man, Jesus, who
has just told you he does not lie to you. . . . What he
said was true. . . . He seems like any other man,
doesn't he? . . . His hair is styled like all the others
at this table. . . . What he wears is no different from
the others. . . . It's his face . . . strong . . . yet
gentle. . . . His eyes that now study your face . . .
seem to look deep into your soul with so much love
that you can feel your heart respond. . . . This Jesus
is the Son of God! . . . Yes . . . how could you doubt
for a minute these words he seems to be speaking to
you personally. . . .

Jesus continues to speak, "Whoever loves me
will obey my teachings, and my Father will love you
and my Father and I will come and live with you. . .
I love you just as the Father loves me." . . . Jesus
pauses. . . . Take this moment and try to grasp what
Jesus has just told you. . . . Jesus loves you . . .
yes, you . . . just as the Father loves him! . . . If this
were not so, Jesus wouldn't have said it, would he?
Jesus touches your hand to get your attention. . . .
He calls you by name . . . "and, I chose you. . . .
My Father will give you whatever you ask in my
name . . . for the Father Himself loves you."

Jesus stands . . . raises his eyes and arms toward heaven and begins to pray, "Father, keep them safe by the power of your name . . . so that they may be one just as you and I are one. . . . I do not ask you to take them out of the world but I ask you to keep them safe from evil . . . and, for their sake, I dedicate myself to you, in order that they too may be truly dedicated to you. . . . I made you known to them, and I will continue to do so . . . in order that the love you have for me may be in them . . . and so that I also may be in them."

Jesus sits . . . turns to you. . . . See the tears in his eyes. . . . Take your fingers and touch his tears. . . . Feel the wetness on your fingertips. . . . Jesus takes your hand in his and says, "I must go now to lay down my life for you. . . . It is my Father's will. . . . Do you still doubt my everlasting love for you?"

I will leave you in silence to allow this blessed moment to stay with you . . . so that you can continue to be in the love of Jesus that is being poured out on you.

Prayer

Jesus, I will never doubt again your love for me, nor question your love when I feel unlovable and that no one loves me. When I feel weak and ready to give up, I will come to you and open my heart to your love for me to give me courage and strength to keep your commandment, "To love one another as you have loved me." Amen. (Invite spontaneous prayer.)

It is time to leave. It may be hard, for I know that you would like to stay a while longer, but remember, you can always come back and be enfolded in Jesus' love for you. Say good-bye. Get up and begin to walk out of the room. Feel Jesus' love follow you. Open your eyes and come back into this room.

Journal Writing

While you are still quiet within, write down any thoughts or feelings you had during this meditation.

Sharing

(It is suggested that the sharing take place is small groups.) Jesus' words in this meditation were taken from the Scriptures. Were they hard to believe?

■ Did you have any doubts about what Jesus said to you? It is important not only to share your doubts with each other but to try to find out why you doubt.

■ What are ways you can lessen these doubts and eventually banish them so that you can begin to really believe and realize that Jesus' words are true and are for you personally?

■ Would realizing Jesus' love for you affect the way you live? How?

■ Jesus' last commandment—to love one another as he loves us—is a tough commandment. Why?

■ How would one go about practicing this commandment? Maybe before we answer this we need to clarify what loving someone else means.

■ How would this practice affect our relationship with others?

■ Does Jesus expect us to go out and do this on our own? What about those that don't like us or who irritate us? Can we actually reach out in love to them?

Activity

1. With class input, list on the board situations in which it would be hard to practice Jesus' commandment (family, school, sports, work, peer group, friends).

2. Next to each situation, have class list ways to reach out in love.

3. Have someone copy the list and attach it to a bulletin board titled "Love One Another As I Have Loved You."

4. In preparation for the liturgy, have each person write on a slip of paper one possible difficult situation.

Liturgy

1.   During the offertory at the Eucharistic Liturgy each person takes her or his piece of paper and lays it on the altar (or burns it in a brazier that is set before the altar) saying, "Jesus, I give this to you. Thank you for helping me."

2.   In the classroom gather the class around the Bible and Christ candle. Invite class members to quietly go back to the upper room and be with Jesus. After a minute of silence, each person is invited to place his or her piece of paper on the Bible, saying, "Jesus, I give this to you. Thank you for helping me."

Prayer of Praise and Thanksgiving

(Use meditation music during prayer.)
Response: "We praise and thank you, Jesus."

For loving us the way you do (Response)
For laying down your life for us (Response)
For showing us the way to you (Response)
For being our strength as we reach out to others
     (Response)
(Invite students to add their own petitions.)

Sing *Yahweh, I Know You Are Near.*

Suggested Music: *In Memory of Jesus* by Carey Landry (NALR); *Bread of Life* by Rory Cooney (NALR).

Loneliness

"Come to Me and Rest"
Matthew 11:25–28

Teacher Introduction

If I told you that we all get to be lonely today, would you be excited and happy? Why not? Is there a difference between being alone and being lonely? Do you think that everyone experiences loneliness at one time or another? What do you think causes the feeling of loneliness? What would be your definition of loneliness? Give some examples of a loneliness experience, either from your own life or from what you might have observed in someone else's life. Can we always escape this experience? Name groups of people in our society whom you suspect are very lonely. This is not an easy topic, is it? In fact, it is an uncomfortable one. Why?

There would have been experiences of loneliness in Jesus' life, too. Think about it. Jesus was a person on the fringe of society because of his teachings which threatened important people. He was rejected and misunderstood. We forget that

27

Jesus also left the security of home, the love and acceptance of his mother, and the familiar faces and places of his home town. Therefore, Jesus did suffer from loneliness at times in his life.

We are going to be with Jesus when he has just gone through a rejection experience, one that would cause any human being to feel isolated. Even though Jesus was with those who loved and supported him, he knew that they did not understand who he really was.

Meditation

Close your eyes. . . .Take a deep breath. . . . Relax. . . . You are outside a town and sitting under a shade tree with Jesus. . . . The day is hot . . . and the shade from this tree offers some relief. . . . Sit very still. . . . Can you feel the slight breeze that ever-so-often touches your face? . . . It feels good, doesn't it? . . . It's not easy being on the road day after day . . . going from town to town. . . . It's good to enjoy times like this . . . resting with Jesus and his followers. . . . But study the faces of the apostles. . . . Did you ever see such unhappy faces? . . . Look at Peter . . . his frown . . . his turned-down mouth. . . . Listen to his deep sighs. . . . Some of the apostles are not sitting but are aimlessly wandering around. . . .Jesus is unusually silent. . . . What is happening here? . . . John sits down beside you and tries to explain, "After all of the work Jesus did to help the people in that town, they haven't even tried to change their lives. . . . It's as if Jesus never even taught them." . . . Philip walks up . . .

greets you by name . . . and adds, "If it were just this town, but there have been so many towns."

Jesus has been silent . . . listening to John and Philip. . . . He now stands . . . walks a short distance away . . . and begins to pray. . . . Philip stops talking . . . watches Jesus for a moment . . . gets up . . . motions to you to follow him . . . and together you join the others gathering around Jesus. Listen to Jesus' prayer, "Father, Lord of heaven and earth, I thank you because you have shown to the unlearned what you have hidden from the wise and learned. . . . Yes, Father, this was how you were pleased to have it happen."

Jesus turns . . . looks at you and the apostles. "My Father has given me all things," he tells you, and gestures towards the trees and the flower-filled fields around you. He continues . . . but his voice seems sad, "No one knows the Son except the Father." . . . If no one really knows Jesus, then he must at times feel lonely, don't you think? . . . It is something to think about, isn't it? . . . Your own life experience of being misunderstood . . . no one really understanding your feelings . . . your needs. . . . Jesus looks at you . . . calls you by name. . . . Walk over to him. . . . Allow him to take your hands in his. . . . Feel the strength of Jesus' hands . . . the comfort within you . . . the peace in this personal touch of Jesus who looks deeply into your eyes. Let his healing power fill your soul with an inner peace. . . . No, don't lower your eyes. . . . Let them look deeply into the love for you that fills Jesus' eyes and face. . . . "Come to me," Jesus says, "I know you are tired from carrying burdens, especially the burden of loneliness. . . . I understand. . . . Let me give you rest." . . . Jesus begins to walk . . . still holding your hand in his. . . . "For with me your burden will be light," Jesus says. . . . You have come to a large shade tree. . . . Jesus sits down and gently pulls you down next to him. . . . Turning, Jesus smiles . . . and says, "When you are lonely, I want you to come to me. . . . For I truly understand this burden we all carry at times. . . . Will you do this . . . come to me at these times?" . . . Jesus waits for you to answer him. I will give you silent time to be alone with Jesus. . . .

Prayer

Jesus, sometimes I am so lonely that I get lost in it and feel that there is no way out. Help me to turn to you at these times. I believe in your words to me and I trust you, for you are my friend and with you this burden will be light. There are so many lonely people in this world, even in the world around me, Jesus. Teach me to forget my own loneliness and reach out to others who are in despair in their loneliness. Help me to bring hope to others. Amen. (Invite spontaneous prayer.)

Journal Writing

Listen to the thoughts and feelings that are in the quiet within you and write them in your journals. You may even feel a prompting within you to reach out to other lonely people. Listen to God's Spirit

within—speaking to you in thoughts and feelings—
listen to the Spirit's prompting.

Sharing

In small groups, invite the class to share their
thoughts and feelings. Allow them to become aware
of a sense of togetherness in this experience, a
bonding in God's Spirit united with theirs.

In the large group, invite anyone who wishes
to do so to share their experience, thoughts, and
possibly an idea that suddenly came to them. (The
discussion should lead into ways of reaching out to
others who are lonely, getting away from self-pity
and becoming aware of the lonely people in our
society.) Ask the class to name groups of lonely
people in today's society. List on the board.

Liturgy (introducing discernment)

Place altar with candle and Bible in front of the
list on the board. Give each class member a slip of
paper and a pencil.

Lead the class back into the presence of Jesus
in their meditation by saying: Let's meet Jesus
again. He is there waiting for you. Listen quietly,
asking the Lord Jesus to guide and help you reach
out to others. Write down any thoughts or ideas that
might come to you during this time on ways to reach
out to others who are lonely.

Have soft meditation music playing in the background. (The *Taizé* tapes are excellent.)

After a few minutes, quietly ask if anyone had any ideas on how to reach out to a lonely person. List on the board. Remind the class that throughout the week ideas might come to them. They should write the ideas down.

Close by having several students each prayerfully recite a verse of *Whatsoever You Do*. Have the rest of the class join in, reciting the chorus after each verse. (As this is happening, individuals should place their written ideas on the Bible.)

Closing song: *You Are Near.*

Activity

Design a reaching-out bulletin board where suggestions (names and activities) can be pinned up throughout the week(s), beginning with the ones placed on the Bible.

The suggested groups of people can either be prayed for each day, and/or the class can decide upon a course of action to reach out to the lonely.

Suggested Music: *I Say Yes, Lord* by Donna Pena (GIA Publications).

All Saints' Day

Visiting the Community of Saints

Teacher Introduction

Have you ever wondered what heaven will be like? What do you imagine it will be like? Jesus often talked about the Kingdom. And the Church continues to teach what Jesus taught—that we are brothers and sisters of Jesus, and heirs of heaven. Even though we believe what the Church teaches, the realization of what it is all about hasn't hit us yet. Maybe it's because we don't have any physical proof, and we are too busy living here.

During the Feast of All Saints is a good time to take a look at what is in store for each of us. Now is a good time to think and pray about that. So we are going to place ourselves in the "vestibule" of heaven, and look around. We will try to experience what it could possibly be like. Let's open our hearts and minds to God's grace and love.

Meditation

Close your eyes. . . . Take a deep breath . . . and relax. . . . You're in a place we will call the "vestibule of heaven." . . . The first thing you begin to feel is the weightlessness . . . the burden of ordinary living being lifted from you. . . . Feel this weight leaving you. . . . Experience that. . . . Now feel the peace of knowing that it is great to be just who you are . . . no more excuses . . . no guilt for just being you. . . . Begin to experience the hominess . . . a sense of belonging. . . . This is where you are meant to be eventually. . . . Slowly, a peace begins to fill your whole being. . . . Let this peace flow through you. . . . A feeling of joy now begins to come over you . . . like one big happy smile all through you. . . . Stay with this for a moment. . . . Enjoy. . . .

Someone is coming toward you. . . . It's Peter. . . . Maybe he really is this gatekeeper we joke about. . . . He embraces you with a welcome hug. . . . His eyes shine with the joy of seeing you. . . . "Welcome home!" he tells you. "Come," he says and takes you by the hand. . . . "There are many waiting to see you . . . especially a certain few." He leads you to Mary, Jesus' mother. . . . Mary sees you and her arms open up to greet you. . . . Go into her arms. . . . Listen to her joyous words of welcome. . . . Feel her mother's love . . . unconditional love . . . flow through you. . . . Others are now gathering around you . . . greeting you. . . . Experience their love and acceptance . . . and their welcoming joy. . . . There is someone very

34

special who waits for you to turn and recognize him . . . yes, your friend Jesus. . . . He laughs . . . speaks your name . . . holds open his arms to you. . . . Run into Jesus' welcoming arms . . . the arms of love . . . the arms of Jesus. . . . Go ahead, express yourself . . . the way you have always wanted to when you were happy. . . . Don't hold back or be embarrassed. . . . You are totally accepted here . . . for the unique person you are. . . . Feel the warmth of Jesus' love and peace fill you . . . the protection of his whole being united to yours. . . . How could you ever doubt again Jesus' love for you? . . . What an experience! . . . Isn't it great to be here?

More people of God gather around you. . . . They all seem to want to share with you. . . . Someone comes forward . . . smiles . . . . pats your shoulder and says, "We understand. . . . We have also struggled." . . . Do you recognize him? . . . It's Joseph, the father of Jesus. . . . Another person comes up excitedly, almost shouting, "Keep running that race. . . . Don't give up. . . . We're betting on you." Yes, it's Paul. . . . He still has the same personality you have often read of or heard about. . . . Then someone says, "It all has to do with love." . . . It has to be John, the beloved disciple of Jesus because he always preached about love. . . . He smiles at you. . . . Yes, it is John. . . . A young woman comes up to you . . . places her hand on your arm . . . smiles and says, "Call on me sometimes. I would love to help you." . . . It's St. Therese, called the Little Flower. . . . So many beautiful people opening themselves up to you . . .

so willing to help. . . . In fact, look around. . . . Everyone is happy to see you . . . welcoming you . . . encouraging you. . . . There is no selfish reason here for reaching out to you. . . . They really care . . . asking questions about your life, your hobbies, your friends. . . . Jesus takes your hand in his . . . smiles and tells you, "Remember, I am always with you. . . . My strength is with you. . . . My life on earth was all for you. Will you believe this?" . . . What would you like to say to Jesus . . . to the saints? . . . I'll give you this time to be with them.

Prayer

Jesus, this is an overwhelming experience for me to be here with you and all your friends and to learn that they are also my friends. Thank you for this moment to experience the promise of your Kingdom, to have it become more real to me. Knowing that your love and strength are always with me, I will run the race as Paul said, and not give up. Amen. (Invite spontaneous prayer.)

Everyone knows it is time for you to leave. They keep assuring you of their help. "Just call on us. We'll be there!" someone calls out. Say your good-byes. This visit is too short, I know. But you can always return. Begin to walk away. Open your eyes, and come back into the room.

Journal Writing

Write down your experience, thoughts, or feelings from this meditation.

Sharing

In small groups, have students share thoughts and feelings they had during the meditation.

Discussion

Read the life of a modern saint, or of someone who has lived a life that was exemplary.

Follow-up questions:

■ What were some of the good qualities you noticed about this person? (List on board.)

■ How did these qualities influence others? The world at large?

■ Were there any traits that you questioned, wondering how that person could be called a saint or hero with traits like that?

■ Were you aware of struggles, surface struggles as well as deeper personal struggles?

■ Was there any happiness, joy, fun in this person's life? Is this important? Why or why not?

■ Would you like to have known this person? Have this person as a friend?

■ Could this person be an example for you? Give your reasons.

Activity

Have the class gradually develop a bulletin board of names/pictures of people they admire. Underneath each picture post one quality about that person that can be admired.

Liturgy

If this meditation is on or near All Saints' Day, the Eucharistic celebration would be an excellent closing. Have the class plan the Liturgy.

Para-Liturgy

Preparation: On an altar place a Bible, a Christ candle, special bread, and a goblet of grape juice.

The love of Jesus for you and me is unlimited, unconditional, something that most of us find so hard to comprehend. All we can do is say, "Yes, I believe" and then celebrate this magnificent love of Jesus for us! What better way to do this than celebrate his words of love for us in the breaking of the bread and drinking of the cup of salvation, reliving the Eucharistic celebration of Jesus' Last Supper on earth.

(Read Mark 14:22–23.) "While they were eating, Jesus took a piece of bread, gave a prayer of thanks, broke it, and gave it to his disciples. 'Take it,' he said, 'this is my body.' " (Pass the bread to the students and invite them to break a piece off and pass it to the next person.)

"Then he took a cup, gave thanks to God, and handed it to them; 'This is my blood which is poured out for many, my blood which seals God's covenant.' " (Pass the cup of grape juice to the students.)

Play the song *Hosea,* and all quietly listen. When the song is finished, hold hands and pray the Lord's Prayer together.

Suggested Music: *Canticle of the Sun* by Marty Haugen (GIA Publications); *Great Is the Lord* by Suzanne Toolan, S.M. (GIA Publications); *Though the Mountains May Fall* by Dan Schutte, S.J. (NALR).

Why Does God Let This Happen?

Mary: Journey to Bethlehem Luke 1:1–6

Preparation

Have available newspaper clippings covering the subject of the tragedies and suffering in the local community and in the world today (war, homelessness, poverty, hunger, violence, drugs, materialism, child abuse, etc.).

Discussion

Discuss the articles and also let the young people share personal tragedies and suffering. Ask leading questions such as: Where is God in all of this? Is God responsible for what is happening in our world today? Do we blame God? Why or why not? What are we doing about all of this? What else can we do?

Have the students write down what they honestly believe and give reasons for their statements. (Either collect the papers or have the students keep their statements in a safe place for future use. After the third meditation, they will be asked the same questions and will compare these responses to their first statements.)

Now let's look at three people—Jesus, Mary, and Joseph. They suffered too—a great deal. We will be going into Scripture scenes and become personally involved in specific situations in the lives of Jesus, Mary, and Joseph—as we seek to find answers to our question, "Why does God let this happen?"

Teacher Introduction

We are first going to be with Mary and Joseph as they travel from Nazareth to Bethlehem, a seventy-to-eighty mile walk. Mary is in her ninth month of pregnancy, a most uncomfortable time for any mother-to-be. They have to go, for the Emperor Augustus wants a census and everyone is ordered to go to their hometown to register. Mary and Joseph have to register in Bethlehem because Joseph was of the family of King David who had lived in Bethlehem.

Meditation

Close your eyes. . . . Take a deep breath and relax. . . . Any concerns or distractions you might have, give to the Lord . . . for this is a very special time for you.

41

You are on a road walking with Mary and Joseph. . . . Your destination is Bethlehem. . . . It is the third day of a long, hard dusty trip. . . . Your feet are sore . . . and you are tired. . . . Sleeping on the ground for two nights wasn't exactly restful. . . . The sun seems to be extra hot on you. . . . Feel its rays beating down on your head, your shoulders. . . . Look around and see the dry rocky land around you. . . . Notice that you have been traveling with a large group. . . . People travel in groups as it is dangerous to travel alone on this road. . . . There are many robbers around who would attack you. . . . Listen to the grumblings of these people. . . . They are complaining about being forced to go to Bethlehem . . . about the heat . . . about many things . . . a disgruntled crowd it seems. . . . It doesn't help the situation, does it?

You are walking beside a donkey which is carrying Mary. . . . Joseph is leading the donkey. Place your hand on the donkey. . . . Feel the hot, damp hide. . . . Joseph turns to you. . . . His face is wet with perspiration . . . and his eyes are tired and filled with concern. . . . "Hold on to Mary. The road is rough up ahead," he tells you as he glances from you to Mary. . . . Mary has been silent for a long time now. . . . Feel the peace about her . . . but at the same time notice that she bites her lip from time to time. . . . From pain? . . . From discomfort? . . . Is her baby going to be delivered while traveling? . . . Allow concern for Mary to flow through you. . . . Enter more into this scene. . . . Be aware of Joseph's concern. . . . Hold on to Mary tightly. . . . What else can you do? . . . It's a hopeless situation, isn't it? . . . Mary touches your shoulder . . . smiles down at you. . . . "It will be all right," she tells you. "God is with us." . . . She seems so uncomfortable . . . yet there is a calmness about her. . . .

Listen to the questions in your heart. . . . Feel the frustration of this entire situation that Joseph, Mary, and you seem to be stuck in. . . . Why isn't she complaining like the others? . . . Of all people, she has every right to question God. . . . And where is this God that Mary seems to rely on? . . . Why is God allowing all this to happen? . . . Mary is such a good person. . . . Is this God's will? . . . Can it be that God is a cruel God?

This is your time now. . . . Continue to walk with Mary. . . . Ask your questions . . . and listen. . . . In a few minutes I will lead you away from Mary and Joseph and bring you back into this room. (Allow a few minutes of silence.)

Prayer

Mary, it is time for me to leave. I've tried to listen, to understand about God's will and why God allowed this to happen to you and Joseph—and to somehow understand God's will in the terrible tragedies in this world today. Help me to have peace and calm, knowing that God is taking care of me. Amen. (Invite spontaneous prayer.)

Say good-bye to Mary and Joseph. Turn and begin to walk down the road away from them. Open your eyes and come back into this room.

43

Journal Writing

Write down any thoughts or questions that come to you during the meditation, and during your silent time. For we are learning to listen to God's Spirit within us. This is an important time for you.

Suggested Music: *Come Set Us Free* by B. Farrell (St. Thomas Moore Center).

Why Does God Let This Happen?

Joseph: Flight into Egypt
Matthew 2:1–18

Teacher Introduction

In an effort to find answers to our question, "Why does God let this happen?" we are going to study Joseph's reaction to a traumatic situation in his life—the flight into Egypt. (Read Matthew 2:1–18.) We can approach our answers from a human standpoint as well as from a Divine standpoint, for Joseph was a human being who had the same needs and desires as we do today. It may help us appreciate what Joseph was going through if we keep in mind that the culture of his time was insistent that the man is the provider and protector of his family.

Women obeyed their husbands, raised the children, and took care of the home. They did not have jobs outside of the home. Therefore, when we enter into this meditation, some of us might have to readjust our thinking about the roles of husbands and wives.

Meditation

Close your eyes. . . . Take a deep breath and relax. . . . Place yourself on a desert road. . . . All is emptiness. . . . Any breeze that you experience also blows sand into your eyes . . . stinging your face. . . . The sun is beating down unmercifully on your head . . . penetrating your clothes . . . and perspiration covers your entire body. . . . Take a moment to become aware of the fact that you are terribly uncomfortable. . . . This desert walk is not a pleasant one, is it? . . . You have every right to complain. . . . However . . . the man next to you is silent. . . . He seems to accept the hardship that this desert persistently offers. . . . When he does speak it is of selfless encouragement to Mary, his wife . . . their child . . . and to you. . . . Look at his face. . . . The man is Joseph. . . . Notice the sand sticking to his beard . . . to his face . . . glued there by perspiration. . . . Touch your own face. . . . Feel the gritty sand covering it. . . . And there is no relief in sight. . . .

Joseph stops . . . gives you the reins to the donkey that carries not only their few belongings and jugs of water, but also the child Jesus. . . . "We need to stop for water," he tells you. . . . "Just hold this poor old donkey still." He turns toward Jesus and Mary and smiles. . . . Watch him unstrap a water jug . . . pour some water in a clay cup and give it to Mary. . . . She quietly takes the cup and helps Jesus drink the water. . . . It's like a sacred ritual of life. . . . No one says anything as each gently takes the cup. . . . Not one drop is spilled.

. . . Joseph gives you the cup. . . . Feel the coolness of the water as you drink. . . . It is refreshing and reviving, isn't it? . . . Watch as Joseph pours some water into a leather pouch and holds it for the donkey to drink. . . . "Poor animal is really thirsty," Joseph says to you over his shoulder.

You continue your journey into Egypt. . . . Each step brings you closer to safety, away from Herod who is most likely right at this moment sending his soldiers out to kill all male children two-years-old and younger. . . . Feel the gratefulness within you for the safety of this special family you are growing to love as you listen to Mary quietly talking to Jesus . . . entertaining him. . . . Hear his childish laughter in response. . . . Joseph looks back at them . . . smiles. . . . He glances at you . . . shakes his head . . . his eyes filled with concern and he says, "They are so vulnerable to life . . . the elements . . . depending on me to protect them and lead them to safety." . . . He sighs. "And those innocent children . . . being slaughtered, most likely right now as I am speaking . . . for what? . . . A mad man's desire to make sure of his power?" . . . Joseph gestures toward Jesus . . . and looks at you. . . . There is a spark of anger in his eyes as he goes on, "Is this child a threat to that mad man? . . . Look at him. . . . Why?"

"We're homeless again," Joseph seems now to be talking to himself . . . "uprooted because of Herod!" . . . It's easy to question God now, isn't it? . . . Is this how God treats those who are loyal to Him? Is God just? . . . Why does He allow this to

happen to these good people? . . . Turn to Joseph.
. . . Maybe he can help you with these questions
. . . but wait . . . he seems to be deep in prayer.
. . . You can make out a few words of a Psalm. . . .
''He alone protects and saves me, he is my defender,
and I shall no longer be defeated.'' (Psalm 62) . . .
Does prayer really help? . . . Does it work? . . . How
can Joseph turn to a God who lets this happen to
him? . . .

Continue to walk next to Joseph through this
merciless desert. . . . Go ahead and ask Joseph the
questions you have . . . and, most of all, listen. . . .
I will give you a silent time for this. (Give the
students a few minutes of silence. Watch for
restlessness.)

Prayer

Joseph, help me to see God's will in all of
this—your homelessness, the hardship of trudging
through this desert, your concern for your family, the
merciless slaughter of innocent children. I do not
understand why God allows this to happen. Help me
to walk with God in the blind faith that you and Mary
experienced, trusting totally in God's love for me.
Amen. (Invite spontaneous prayer.)

It is time to leave Joseph and his family. Say
good-bye. Turn and begin to walk away. Open your
eyes and come back into the room.

Journal Writing

It is important to write down any thought you might have had during this meditation, as we search for an answer to our question, "Why does God let this happen?" For we are learning to listen and discern God's Spirit guiding us and giving us new life.

Suggested Music: *Don't Give Up On What?* by Ron Griffen (Leaven Productions); *As Water to the Thirsty* by David Haas (GIA Publications); *He Calls Us Each by Name* by Ron Griffen (Leaven Productions); *You Are Near* by Dan Schutte, S.J. (NALR).

Why Does God Allow This to Happen?

Jesus:Jesus Before the Sanhedrin
Mark 14:53–65;
Matthew 26:57–75;
Luke 22:54–71

Teacher Introduction

This meditation will be a challenge to us. It might even be disturbing as it opens our eyes to situations in the world, possibly in our own world — conditions that are uncomfortable to recognize. For example, how do you feel about apartheid in Africa, the slaughters in El Salvador, the power of one man in Iraq? And what about right around us, the drive-by shootings, the homeless and starving children? In your own lives, do you see any injustices around you? Why does God allow this to happen?

In Jesus' life these injustices were also going on. Jesus is God but he was also human and had human reactions. He knew that he had come to do his Father's will — to bring the good news of salvation to all who would listen. His message disturbed and threatened many, especially the ruling class of the Jews. But he continued to do the work he was sent to do, knowing that the rulers of the Jews were out to get him . . . and they did. Jesus was betrayed and arrested.

Injustices of those in power, a trial at night which was illegal, held in the house of the high priest, again illegal (all trials had to be held in the court), false witnesses. Are any of these injustices familiar in our lives today? Why does God allow this to happen to His own Son?

Meditation

I am going to lead you into meditation and we are going to experience Jesus' illegal trial by night. . . . Close your eyes. . . . Take a deep breath . . . and relax. . . .

You are standing behind a marble pillar in a large hall. . . . The ceiling is twice as high as that of a normal room. . . . The floor is stone. . . . There are many marble pillars like the one you are standing behind. . . . Look to your right. . . . There is a large group of men. . . . They are the ruling body of the Jews . . . the Sanhedrin . . . very powerful. . . . Notice that one man seems to be the center of attention. . . . He is the high priest. His name is Caiaphas. . . . These men seem to be excited. . . . Look at the way they wave their hands as they almost yell at each other . . . their eyes darting toward a large doorway closed off by bronze double doors. . . . Look straight ahead. . . . Those nervous looking men being guarded are the false witnesses. . . . The entire hall seems chaotic. . . . Feel the unrest here. . . .

Suddenly, there is silence. . . . All eyes turn toward the bronze doors that are slowly being opened. . . . Listen to their hinges squeak and echo through the hall. . . . Look! . . . Two guards are leading a man whose hands are tied behind his back. . . . It is the prisoner—Jesus! . . . He walks slowly and with dignity . . . eyes straight ahead . . . directed toward the high priest. . . . He now stands in the center of the hall. . . . The guards retreat . . . leaving Jesus alone and vulnerable to the whims of the Sanhedrin. . . . Do you wonder where his friends are? . . . Especially those who followed him for three years? . . . How do you feel about this? . . .

The high priest begins to question Jesus. . . . Jesus remains silent. . . . The witnesses stumble forth now. . . . Each gives Jesus a quick look . . . but turns away from him. One witness tells the high priest, "He said, 'I will tear down this Temple which men have made, and after three days I will build one that is not made by men!' " . . . Feel your anger. . . . The witness twisted Jesus' words! . . . Another witness . . . and still another witness is called out. . . . Watch them. . . . They seem nervous, don't they? . . . Listen as they contradict each other's story. . . . Feel hope rise within you. . . . No one can prove that Jesus is guilty of anything. . . . The high priest becomes impatient . . . stands. . . . With one hand he waves the witnesses away. . . . With the other he points to Jesus. . . . His voice trembles as he almost shouts, "Are you the Messiah, Son of the Blessed God?" . . . Unfair!!! . . . The question is illegal. . . . It is not allowed by law to ask incriminating questions. . . . The silence is heavy. . . . All eyes are on Jesus . . . waiting for his response. . . . He could twist his answer in some way so as not to incriminate himself. . . . You wait. . . . Feel your heart pound. . . . Jesus, for the first time, speaks, "I am." . . . He's done for. . . . Just what the high priest was waiting for. . . . The high priest rips his garments . . . the official response to blasphemy . . . "We don't need any more witnesses!" he shouts. "You heard his blasphemy. . . . What is your decision?" . . . Let your emotions respond to the misuse of justice . . . the evil here. . . . Feel anger, despair. . . . And the verdict is passed . . . death to the prisoner.

Look! Witnesses and servants are rushing up to Jesus . . . spitting on him . . . calling him names . . . and slapping his face. . . . This gentle person who loved people so much . . . and the guards let them do this! . . . The high priest orders the guards to take Jesus away. . . . The guards jerk Jesus around . . . toward another entrance. . . . They lead him past you . . . and for a moment Jesus turns and looks at you . . . his face now bruised and covered with spittle. . . . His heart speaks to your heart. . . . Listen, what is it that Jesus is saying to you? . . . What do you want to say to Jesus? . . .

Take this time of quiet and stay with Jesus here in the hall. . . . Let his eyes meet yours. . . . Listen. . . .

Prayer

Jesus, I don't understand why all this had to happen to you. You stood up for what you believed in. You did what your Father wanted you to do and, yet, look what happened to you! What are you teaching me though this, Jesus? Help me to listen to your Spirit within me, and give me courage and strength that will get me through times when I feel so vulnerable to temptations around me. Help me, Jesus, to open up my heart to your love, guidance, and strength. For there are many things I do not understand about God's will in my life. All I know right now is that I love you and trust in your love for me. Amen. (Invite spontaneous prayer.)

It's time to leave. Jesus is being lead away now. Begin to walk out of the hall. Turn and look at Jesus once more as he is being led out of this hall. Open your eyes and come back into the room.

Journal Writing

It is important to write down any thoughts that you had during this meditation. Be quiet within. Listen to the movement of God's Spirit within you, and write. This is an important time for you.

Sharing

Pass out the students' first responses to the question, "Why does God allow this to happen?" Give them time to respond to this question again.

Form small groups and have the students compare their first and second responses and give reasons why they changed their answers, or why they did not change their answers.

A general class discussion can follow.

Activity

Draw a large tree with many branches. On the branches, place the original clippings from newspapers you brought in. The class can add more, writing down injustices and suffering they see around them and in the world.

Through a class discussion decide what the students could do to help others in this world of suffering and injustice. Keep it practical and simple. Write these decisions on paper and place in the center of paper flowers to be attached to the tree. Have the students write their names on the leaves.

Choose a quote from Jesus to be written on the tree truck during the closing prayer. "Come to me all you who are burdened and I will refresh you," "Love one another as I love you," or another quote could be used. Let the class choose.

You now have a Tree of Life. Where there was hopelessness, now there is hope—because we are our brothers' and sisters' keeper.

Closing Prayer

(During the prayer service, write the quote from Jesus on the tree trunk and place the flowers and leaves on the tree. Place the Bible, the candle, and the tree together.)

Read aloud Luke 19:1–12 or Luke 9:1–6 about discipleship.

As music is played, have each student place his or her name leaf and flower on the tree.

Close by joining hands and reciting together the Lord's Prayer, or the Prayer of St. Francis, or a prayer that one of the students has written.

Suggested Music: *Come Set Us Free* by B. Farrell (St. Thomas Moore Center); *We Remember* (by Marty Haugen (GIA Publications).

Who Am I?

"Who Do People Say That I Am?"
Luke 9:18–20

Teacher Introduction

Do you often wonder about yourself—who you are? Why were you born? Do you base your identity on what other people say about you? Down deep, do you feel that people really don't know you—the real you?—even your parents? Are you so busy trying to please others that you get confused about who you are, what you like, what you don't like, how you feel about things?

Jesus also wondered what other people thought of his identity. Could it be that the human Jesus also had to struggle like you, because of outside forces? First, he's praised and then he's rejected. Even his close friends, the apostles, didn't seem to know who Jesus really was nor understand him. Does this sound familiar to you?

We will be looking at the life of Jesus, meeting him in various scenes of the Scripture, and learning how Jesus handled rejection and praise. These are situations that are familiar to us and confuse our self-knowledge.

Meditation

In our struggle for self-identity, let's be with Jesus when he questioned his close friends the apostles about just this.

Close your eyes. . . . Take a deep breath and relax. . . . You are seated under a shade tree in the country with the twelve apostles waiting for Jesus who went off by himself to pray. . . . It is so peaceful here. . . . Listen to the quiet. . . . You can hear the sounds of the country . . . birds chirping above you . . . the gentle rustle of leaves. . . . Hear the song of the crickets. . . . It's peaceful being away from the cities and towns and crowds of people who make demands on Jesus all day. . . . Take a deep breath and enjoy the smells of the country . . . the perfume of the blue and yellow wildflowers scattered throughout the fields. . . .

Peter breaks the silence. . . . He stands . . . stretches . . . and mumbles something about finding Jesus and getting going. . . . Feel your reluctance to move. . . . The countryside seems to have cast a lazy, dreamy spell over you. . . . Peter leads the way and all of you follow him to a clump of trees in the field just ahead. . . . Jesus is seated under a tree overlooking a cliff. . . . He sees you coming . . . watches as you make your way through the field toward him. . . . And, before Peter can say anything,

58

Jesus says, "Come sit down for a moment, I have something to ask you." . . . Go over and sit next to Jesus. . . . It's a good place to be, isn't it? . . . Jesus places his arm around your shoulders and gives you a hug. "I'm glad you came," he tells you.

Jesus now looks at each of you . . .sighs . . . and slowly asks, "Who do the crowds say that I am?" . . . Is this your question, too? . . . Wanting to know what others think of you? . . . Philip frowns . . . thinks a moment and then says, "Some say that you are John the Baptist." . . . Thomas looks at Jesus . . . studies him for a minute and then responds, "Others say that you are Elijah, while others say that one of the prophets of long ago has come back to life." The other apostles seem to agree with Philip and Thomas because they are nodding their heads. . . . They also look puzzled, don't they? . . . Jesus smiles slightly and then asks, "What about you? Who do you say I am?" . . . Peter answers immediately, gesturing his hands as he says, "You are God's Messiah!"

Wonder if Jesus is also struggling with his identity . . . and wanting people to know who he really is. . . . It seems that people have made him out to be who they want him to be . . . not who he really is. . . . You and Jesus have something in common, haven't you? . . . Jesus touches your hand . . . smiles. . . . He seems to have read your thoughts. . . . He quietly speaks your name and asks, "Do you believe that what people say about us changes who we really are?"

I'll give you time now to respond to Jesus and, most importantly, to listen to what he has to say to you.

Prayer

Jesus, so often I feel like a puppet, with other people pulling my strings, trying to make me be and do what they want me to be and do. I know that you didn't let others influence who you really were. You went right ahead doing what you were supposed to do. Help me, Jesus, to do the same. Give me the courage to be the person I was created to be. Amen. (Invite spontaneous prayer.)

It is time to leave Jesus. Say good-bye. Get up and begin to walk away. Open your eyes and come back into the room.

Journal Writing

I will give you time to write down any thoughts you had during this meditation. Try not to think that a certain thought is unimportant . . . write down everything that went through your mind, for we are learning to listen to God's Spirit within us.

Discussion

Would anyone like to share any thoughts or feelings? Did you have any insights about self-identity? What does it mean when we use the term "self-identity?" Is it important to know who you are? How do friends and associates influence what we think about ourselves? Where do you place these outside influences on your value scale? Where do you think Jesus placed them? Why?

Activity

1.   Write down symbols and colors that you think represent who you are.

2.   Write your name (full name or just first name) in a script that would best represent you.

3.   Design a half sheet of paper with your name, symbols, and colors.

Closing Prayer

As the class sits around the Christ candle and the Bible which is opened to Luke 9:18–20, each holding his or her name tag design, have someone read Luke 9:18–20.

Invite the class to return to the scene of the meditation. Allow a minute of quiet so that the class can center.

As each individual places his or her name design by the Bible, they say, "My name is ____. Thank you God for giving me life."

Close with music or join hands and say the Lord's Prayer or a prayer of your choice.

Suggested Music: *Earthen Vessels* by John Foley, S.J. (NALR).

Who Am I?

Believe in Yourself:
The Man with the Paralyzed Hand
Luke 6:6–11

Teacher Introduction

Rejection is not an easy topic to talk about, is it? But everyone experiences it sometime in their life. Can you give me examples of people being rejected in sports or in politics? What other situations could you find yourself in that could possibly lead to a rejection? Are these situations to be avoided? What does rejection do to a person? Is there a way to handle it? Have you experienced or watched someone else stand up for what they believed in and be laughed at? How does one handle a situation like that? Does rejection change who we are?

Jesus experienced quite a bit of rejection during his public life. Did it stop him from continuing his public ministry? He was even rejected by people he knew all his life. One day when Jesus was home visiting his mother on the Sabbath he found himself in a situation where there was a risk of being rejected. Let's become involved in this situation with

63

Jesus and be open to the message that Jesus is teaching each of us in particular.

Meditation

Close your eyes. . . . Take a deep breath . . . and relax. . . . You are in the synagogue with Jesus. . . . Look around and notice that all the men are wearing white shawls over their head. . . . They are called "prayer shawls." . . . It is the Jewish custom for men to wear them when they pray. . . . If you look around, you will see that there are no women here . . . but turn and look up behind you. . . . The women are in a balcony above the room. . . . This is the Jewish custom. . . . The women are separated from the men in the synagogue. . . . Notice that it's taken for granted. . . . No one seems to notice this separation. . . . But there is something happening here today that is not right. . . . Become aware of an uneasy feeling within you. . . . Jesus is standing in front of the assembly. . . . He has just given a teaching. . . . This is not unusual, for a visitor is often asked to do this. . . . There is something else. . . . Look around and study the faces of the men. . . . Up front, to your right, notice that group of men dressed differently than the others. . . . They are the Pharisees and teachers of the Law . . . leaders of the Jewish faith. . . . Their eyes seem to be looking daggers at Jesus. . . . Notice how they act. . . . Their pointing at Jesus and whispering to each other causes those around them to become uneasy. . . . This is what is wrong here, isn't it? . . . Would you expect this to be happening at a time and place set aside to honor God our Father?

But wait! . . . Someone in the congregation is calling Jesus' name. . . . Everyone turns to look at the man. . . . "Jesus, heal my paralyzed hand," he calls out. . . . That gasp you hear is from the Pharisees. . . . See how their eyebrows are raised. . . . They turn quickly to Jesus . . . and wait. . . . Why the surprise gasp? . . . Everyone here has heard about Jesus' miracles. . . . It's the Sabbath! . . . The Law says that no one can work on the Sabbath. . . . It seems that healing is regarded by the Law as work. . . . Watch Jesus. . . . He could not help but see and feel the reaction of the Pharisees and the others. . . . Listen. . . . Now there is total silence. . . . An atmosphere of expectation fills the room. Do you feel it? . . . The man seated next to you nudges you and whispers. . . . "Bet he heals him anyway." . . .

Jesus looks at the man and says, "Stand up and come here to the front." . . . Is he testing the man's courage? . . . Watch the man as he slowly makes his way to Jesus. . . . His eyes do not leave Jesus' face. . . . Jesus watches him . . . then turns to the congregation. . . . His eyes move over the whole room and rest for a moment on the Pharisees. . . . "I ask you," he says, "what does our Law allow us to do on the Sabbath? . . . To help or to harm? . . . To save a man's life . . . or to destroy it?" . . . The man next to you nudges you again and whispers, "He's got us there." . . . Study the Pharisees for a moment. . . . Their faces are like cold stone, aren't they? . . . Enemies for sure. . . . Jesus turns to the man and says, "Stretch out your hand."

. . . Watch the hand! . . . See how the man struggles to stretch his hand toward Jesus. . . . Look! . . . His hand is moving. . . . He is healed! . . . You've just witnessed a miracle!

Listen to the commotion in the room. . . . The Pharisees are standing and shaking their fists at Jesus and yelling out something about breaking the Law. . . . Everyone else is talking at once. . . . Jesus leaves. . . . No one seems to notice. . . . As he passes you, he motions for you to follow him. . . . Get up and hurry after Jesus. . . . At the entrance he waits for his mother who is hurrying down the steps toward him. . . . Jesus places his arm around your shoulder and leads you away from the synagogue. . . . Feel the pressure and strength of Jesus' arm on your shoulder as the three of you walk toward his house. . . . Jesus stops . . . looks into your eyes . . . and asks you, "What do you think I should have done? . . . Played it safe and heal the man in secret? . . . Not threaten the leaders of the Temple who were there?" . . . Jesus continues to walk. . . . He still has his arm on your shoulder. . . . He again stops . . . again turns to you and speaks your name. . . . "Should you and I do what we believe is right . . . what we believe in . . . even though others, even important people, reject us? . . . Does rejection from others have to change who we are?" . . . Jesus waits for your response. I'll give you a quiet time now to speak and listen to Jesus.

Prayer

Jesus, guide me in your ways. I need the grace of your strength and courage when I think I'm being rejected. Rejection hurts and so often lowers my self-esteem. I need people to like me and I am finding out that not everyone does. Give me the wisdom, Lord, to realize that rejection does not change who I am—a person so important in God's eyes as to be created and loved by Him. Thank you for listening, Jesus. Thank you for being my friend. Amen. (Invite spontaneous prayer.)

Journal Writing

As you probably realize, this is an important meditation. Therefore, write down every thought that came to you during the meditation. For we are learning to listen to God's Spirit within us.

Sharing

For your group sharing, use the questions that Jesus asked at the end of the meditation. Divide into small groups. Then come together in the large group to share the responses to the questions.

Activity

Have a copy of Psalm 25 for each member in the class. Read the Psalm and give time for individuals to choose verses that strike them as applying to this meditation.

Have the students rewrite the verse in their own words, keeping to the theme of rejection. Help them begin by giving them an example.

Final Prayer

Gather around the Bible and Christ candle. Have meditative music playing softly. Invite the class to go back to the scene of the meditation. After a minute or two, have each student read his or her Psalm prayer. Close by joining hands and singing *Peace Is Flowing Like a River* or some other appropriate song.

Suggested Music: *Happy Are They Who Believe* by David Haas (GIA Publications).

Who Am I?

Living up to Others' Expectations: *Jesus' Triumphant Entry into Jerusalem*
Matthew 20:1–11; Mark 11:1–11; Luke 19:28–40; John 12:12–19

Teacher Introduction

Living up to the expectations of others can bring a lot of pressure on us, can't it? For example, we are expected to make good grades, or to excel in sports, or to succeed in extracurricular activities, or to be a dependable person. Can you give additional examples of the expectations of others in your life? Do you feel that you have to live up to these expectations? What happens if you don't? What are your feelings when this happens? Do we allow times of recognition or times of failures to influence what we think of ourselves?

We have been following Jesus who has been teaching us about ourselves, to accept who we are and to be glad about it. Let's be with Jesus now, at

69

a time when everyone was glorifying and praising him, to learn what Jesus teaches us about self-identity.

Meditation

Close your eyes. . . . Take a deep breath . . . and relax. . . . You are walking down a road with Jesus and his disciples. . . . Up ahead are the gates leading into the city of Jerusalem. . . . It is the time of the celebration of the Passover and many people are coming to the Temple for this great feast. . . . That is why you see so many people on the road walking toward Jerusalem. Feel the excitement of the people. . . . This is a big celebration time for the Jews.

This should be a time of joy and celebration for everyone you are with. . . . But look at Peter. He is frowning. . . . He looks worried, doesn't he? . . . John sees you studying Peter. . . . He walks over to you. . . . "Peter and all of us are afraid for Jesus' life. . . . He has many enemies here . . . but Jesus is determined to come to Jerusalem." . . . Jesus stops. . . . He walks over to two disciples and says, "Go to the village there ahead of you. As you go in, you will find a colt tied there. He has never been ridden. Untie him and bring him here. If someone asks you why you are untying the colt, tell him that the Master needs him."

The disciples hurry off. . . . Notice how puzzled they look. . . . Jesus turns . . . sees you . . . walks over to you and places his arm around your shoulders. . . . "Come rest with me under that shade tree," he says, as he leads you to the coolness of the shade. . . . Feel the relief from the hot sun. . . . Sit next to Jesus. . . . It's good to rest, to be sitting next to Jesus, isn't it? . . . It's been a long, hot walk. . . . Jesus is silent. . . . Peter sits next to you. . . . He glances at Jesus and frowns . . . but says nothing. . . . Thomas also sits with you. . . . "It's dangerous here," he murmurs. . . . Peter is about to answer, but the two disciples return leading the colt. . . . They bring it to Jesus. . . . "It was just as you said, Jesus," they tell him. . . . Jesus stands . . . walks to the colt. . . . Someone places his cloak over the colt. . . . Jesus mounts the colt, sighs, and says, "Now it is time to enter Jerusalem."

Walk next to Jesus. . . . Place your hand on the colt's neck . . . feel its hot hair and bony neck. . . . Does it know whom it is carrying? . . . Is it aware of the God-man on its back? . . . People are beginning to crowd around you, trying to touch Jesus. . . . Look! . . . Some are tearing palm branches from the trees and laying them in front of the colt. . . . See that man just ahead of you take off his cloak? Watch him. . . . He is laying his cloak in the path of the colt. . . . And the noise! . . . Listen. . . . People are shouting! . . . See if you can make out what they are shouting. . . . "God bless the King who comes in the name of the Lord!" . . . "Peace in heaven and glory to God!" . . . "Hosanna!" . . . Look at Jesus. . . . He smiles at the people . . . but his eyes are sad, aren't they? . . . Someone pushes you aside and taps Jesus on the leg. . . . It's a

Pharisee. . . . "Teacher, command your disciples to be quiet!" he shouts. . . . Jesus looks at him . . . studies his face . . . and then says to the Pharisee, "I tell you that if they keep quiet, the stones themselves will start shouting!" . . . The man gives Jesus an angry look and hurries away. . . .

The colt stops. . . . You have been distracted with everything that is happening. . . . You suddenly realize that you are in front of the Temple. . . . Jesus dismounts the colt . . . places his arm around your shoulder and leads you into the Temple. . . . The disciples are acting as guards and keeping the people from crowding around Jesus. . . . You and Jesus walk toward a large marble pillar. . . . Jesus turns to you . . . studies your face . . . looks back at the crowd being held back by the disciples. . . . "What do you think?" he asks you. "Do those people praise me for who I am or who they want me to be? . . . Or . . . are they caught up in the glory of the moment?" . . . Jesus looks into your eyes, . . . waits for a moment . . . and then asks you another question, "Will they stand by me in my time of disgrace?" . . . He sighs. . . . "People are fickle, you know. . . . Tell me, does what people think of us, either good or bad, change who we really are—inside?" . . . Jesus waits for your response. . . .

I will give you quiet time to be with Jesus.

Prayer

Jesus, I often let what others think of me influence what I think about myself. Help me to listen to your Spirit within me . . . leading me into the knowledge of who I really am. Amen. (Invite spontaneous prayer.)

It is time to leave Jesus. Say good-bye. Begin to walk away. Turn once more toward Jesus. Smile and wave to him. Continue to walk away. Open your eyes and come back into the room.

Journal Writing

Write down any thoughts you had during this meditation. After that, turn back and reread your thoughts from your other two meditations. Then write down any further thoughts you might have. Listen to God's Spirit within speak to you. Do not discount any thought as silly or dumb.

Group Discussion

In small groups, discuss the questions Jesus asked in the meditation. Then come together and share thoughts that came to you from rereading your journal from the other two meditations.

Activity: "False Identity Stones"

Have on hand a large number of stones and black felt-tip markers. (Try to have stones that are large and smooth enough so that students can write a word or phrase on them.)

As the class discusses situations or statements that lead them away from knowing who they really are, have someone write these on the board.

Next, work together on putting these statements in a word or a short phrase that will fit on the stones. Or, write them on a small piece of paper to be wrapped around a stone.

Pass out the stones and markers and have class members write with black felt-tip markers the phrases or words that are meaningful to them on the stones.

Closing Liturgy

In a central place in the room, have the Bible, the lighted Christ candle plus taper candles or some other small candles for each person in the room.

Have the class gather around the Bible. Have quiet music playing in the background.

Say to the class: Jesus told us, "Come to me all that are heavily burdened and I will refresh you . . . for my yoke is sweet and my burden is light." (Or use another appropriate quote from Scripture.)

One by one, take your rock burden and place it before the Bible, giving your burden to Jesus. Then take a candle, light it from the Christ candle, and know that you are indeed a very special person. You are special because you are *you* and you are loved by Jesus, the Light of the World.

Closing song: *We Are the Light of the World.*

Suggested Music: *One Body* by T. Watts/M. O'Brien (Willow Music, Australia).

Journey of Faith

Teacher Introduction

Today we are going to approach the subject of faith. First, what does the word *faith* mean? What is your personal definition and what is the formal meaning as found in a dictionary? What are events we believe in even though we did not witness the events for ourselves? Why do you believe in these events? Whom do you trust when they relate something to you? Why? Is it important to believe in something or someone? What would it be like if we had to have proof in order to believe in anything or anyone? Do you have proof that there is a God? Do you believe in God? Who told you about God? Is there a reason to trust that person?

To step out in blind faith is a risk, isn't it? Today (or for the next few weeks), we are going on a journey of faith and will visit some people of faith. We will make short quiet visits. We won't stay long. The purpose of these visits is to share with them the moment of their blind faith experience as described in the Scriptures and see if their blind faith has affected our lives today.

76

There is another question we need to ask ourselves as we experience these meditations and that is: "Are we being called by God to believe in God and respond to God's call—sometimes in a blind faith—even in the seemingly inconsequential happenings in our everyday lives?

A Road Map for Our
Journey of Faith
(for the teachers)

1.   Do not rush through. One stop a day is enough. Allow time to recapture the experience.

2.   Have the students keep their journals handy, for it is important that they write down their thoughts and impressions while still in the meditation.

3.   Close each meditation with a special prayer and allow for spontaneous prayer.

4.   Allow for small-group discussions so that the students can share their experience. Then, in the large group, center around the people in the meditation and their human and then faith reaction to the circumstances in which they found themselves.

5.   Try not to skip any meditation as there is a certain order to the journey which leads to the Resurrection.

6.   Follow-up activities and a closing para-liturgy are at the end of the sixth journey. Feel free to use this at any time.

Journey of Faith

The Annunciation
Luke 1:26–38

Meditation

Close your eyes. . . . Take a deep breath . . .
and relax. . . . The first stop on our journey of faith
is at Mary's home. . . . She is only about fourteen
years old at this time . . . a young Jewish girl who
loves and trusts God. . . .

You are standing inside a simple room. . . . It
is early morning. . . . The birds are just beginning to
chirp. . . . Feel the freshness of the morning. . . .
Smell the aroma of flowers that permeate this room.
. . . The door is open and casts a triangular light on
the stone floor of the room. . . . A candle is lit and
casts shadows on the walls and ceiling. . . . Take
time to experience this simple room. . . . Look over
there . . . to the far end of the room. . . . Mary is
standing motionless by the candle on the wooden
table. . . . She sees you . . . speaks your name . . .
and stretches out her hand in welcome to you. . . .
Walk over and hold her hand. . . . It is soft, delicate,

and trembling, isn't it? . . . Look at Mary's face . . . it is aglow and her eyes are wide in wonder. . . . "An angel just spoke to me," she confides to you, "and asked me to be the mother of the Messiah." . . . Feel Mary's eyes as she silently watches your reaction. . . . "I said yes," she whispers . . . almost to herself. . . . Mary gently takes her hand out of yours and walks to the doorway and looks out over the countryside. . . . Silently walk with her and stand next to her in the doorway. . . . Experience the peace and wonder of this moment. . . . Just Mary and you . . . silent . . . sharing this overwhelming mystery together . . . in blind faith. I will leave the two of you alone to experience what has just happened. . . . (Allow several minutes of silence.)

It is time to leave Mary wrapped in this God mystery. . . . Silently walk away . . . not disturbing Mary. . . . As you leave, wonder if Mary's blind act of faith and trust in God affected your life today in any way.

Prayer

Mary, this is too much of a mystery for me to understand. Help me to accept God's gift of faith so that I can let go of my doubts and believe. Amen. (Invite spontaneous prayer.)

Journal Writing

(It is important that students have their journals handy so that the prayerful mood is not broken.)

In your silence, turn to your journals and write down any thoughts or feelings you had during the meditation.

Sharing

After the students share their experiences in small groups and then in the large group, ask if they have had any experience in their lives where they had to trust someone without asking questions. Ask if they would call this *blind faith?*

Journey of Faith

The Birth of Jesus
Luke 2:1–7; Matthew 1:24

Meditation

The second stop on our journey of faith is at a cave just outside of Bethlehem. . . . Close your eyes. . . . Take a deep breath . . . and relax. . . . You are standing at the cave entrance. . . . Walk in a few steps and stop to adjust your eyes to the dimness of the cave. . . . There is a light coming from that lantern to your right . . . over there . . . in the back of the cave. . . . Begin to walk in. . . . Feel the straw under your feet. . . . Listen to the sound it makes as your feet brush through it. . . . Now that your eyes are adjusted, look further into the cave . . . toward the back. . . . There is a man and a woman and a baby. . . . See how the lantern's light flickers shadows across their faces? . . . Walk closer. . . . Yes, they are Mary and Joseph. . . . And the baby is Jesus! . . . Here, of all places! . . . See, Mary is seated on a blanket that is on a pile of straw. . . . She is holding her baby, Jesus. . . . Joseph is seated next to them. . . . They are silent . . . caught up in this Mystery. . . . Feel the peace of their silence as they look tenderly at their baby. . . . Jesus looks like any other newborn baby, doesn't he? . . . Small and cuddly. . . . Yet, this baby is God's Son. . . . Mary sees you, smiles, and moves over—inviting you to sit between her and Joseph. . . . Walk over. . . . Sit down by Mary and Joseph. . . . How does it feel to be with these beautiful people? . . . Without a word Mary carefully places her baby in your arms. . . . Her smile invites you to share this moment of mystery with her and Joseph. . . . Feel your heart beat harder. . . . You are being allowed to share this most sacred moment of all with the Son of God when he came to this earth to be with us and live like we do. . . . Open your heart to the wonder of this God moment. . . . Hold Jesus. . . . Allow the peace and awesomeness of what is happening fill you. . . . Feel the joy . . . the peace. I will give you a few minutes of silence just to be here and experience.

Prayer

Mary and Joseph, help me to open my heart to the faith that God wants me to have—to believe and trust in God's love and care for me just as you believe. Amen. (Invite spontaneous prayer time.)

Journal Writing

In silence, write down any thoughts or feelings you had during this meditation.

Sharing

After they have shared their experiences and feelings in small groups and then in the large group, ask the students if they have any questions about God allowing His Son to be born in a cave. Would they have expected otherwise? What would they have expected?

Journey of Faith

The Call of James and John
Matthew 4:18–22

Meditation

Our third stop is on a beach by the Sea of Galilee. . . . Close your eyes. . . . Take a deep breath . . . and relax. . . . Look around. . . . Notice that up ahead are fishing boats pulled onto the shore. . . . One fishing boat has three men in it—an older man and two young men. . . . It's Zebadee and his two sons, James and John. . . . If you look closer, you will see that they are mending their fishing nets. . . . Begin to walk over to them. . . . Feel the cool sand under your feet. . . . It is early morning and the sun has yet to warm the sand. . . . Take a minute to enjoy the beauty of the orange glow of the sky caused by the rising sun. . . . As you walk, listen to the waves swish onto the shore. . . . Watch the sea gulls and listen to their cry as they swoop and circle over the water, looking for food. . . . Smell the freshness of the sea air. . . . It's good to be here, isn't it? . . .

Notice that there is a man walking toward Zebadee and his sons. . . . Do you recognize him? . . . Yes, it is Jesus. . . . He is stopping by the boat and saying something. . . . Walk over, stand beside Jesus and listen. . . . He is speaking to James and John. . . . "Follow me" is all that you hear. . . . Feel those magnetic words of the Lord flow through you. . . . James and John look at Jesus. . . . Notice their faces . . . filled with the joy of recognition, now of love and admiration. . . . They put down their nets, turn to their father, hug him, and whisper something to him. . . . Zebadee slowly nods, looks at Jesus, sadly smiles, sighs, and watches his two sons climb out of the boat, leave him, and walk toward Jesus. . . . What must Zebadee be thinking? . . . Jesus, James, and John slowly and silently walk down the beach, away from Zebadee. . . . You join them. . . . Don't try to say anything . . . just walk quietly beside them.

Experience this moment . . . two grown men leaving home . . . leaving their father alone . . . to follow Jesus . . . To where? . . . To what? . . . Do they know? . . . Is this blind faith? . . . Could you do this? . . . Could you risk everything . . . jump into the unknown . . . not knowing what lies ahead? . . . Has the response of James and John affected your life today? . . . Continue to walk silently with Jesus, James, and John down the beach. . . . I will give you a few minutes of silence to experience this moment of mystery.

Prayer

Jesus, is this what you ask of us, blind trust in you? I don't know if I could ever do this, Lord. If I took time to be quiet and listen to you I think that I would hear your call to me to let go of the little daily things that happen in my life. But do I want to? Am I afraid to let go? Lord Jesus, I need your strength to do this. Help me, Lord, to say yes to you in the little things you ask in my everyday life. Amen. (Invite spontaneous prayer.)

It's time to leave. Silently walk away. Open your eyes and come back into the room.

Journal Writing

Write your thoughts and feelings in your journal—your response to this situation.

Sharing

After the class members have shared their feelings and thoughts in small groups and then in the larger group, ask them to respond to the question, "How does the blind trust and faith of James and John affect our lives today? What are the little everyday things in our lives that we hold onto?

Journey of Faith

The Roman Officer
Luke 7:1–10; Matthew 8:5

Meditation

The fourth stop on our journey of faith is with Jesus during his public life. . . . Close your eyes. . . . Take a deep breath . . . and relax. . . .

You are with Jesus and his disciples on a dusty road leading to Capernaum. . . . It is midday and the sun is hot. . . . Feel its heat on your head . . . the hot dust from the road on your feet. . . . Peter wipes the sweat from his face with his sleeve . . . and then points ahead and smiles. . . . Look, people are hurrying toward you. . . . Children are running ahead of the group of people and calling, "Jesus! . . . Jesus!" . . . Jesus stops. . . . He smiles . . . stoops down and holds his arms open to welcome the children. . . . Watch as they crash into his arms . . . almost knocking him over. . . . Jesus catches his balance . . . throws back his head, laughs and hugs them. . . . See how he enjoys these children! . . . Listen to the greetings as disciples and friends meet. . . . This is a happy occasion, isn't it?

. . . Capernaum is Jesus' home base. . . . He and his disciples are most welcome here. . . .

Notice that a man is pushing his way through the crowd. . . . People are making room for him . . . out of respect. . . . Peter tells you that he is an elder in the community. . . . The man now stands facing Jesus. . . . He quickly begins to tell Jesus that a Roman officer's servant is sick. . . . "The man really deserves your help," he pleads. . . ."He loves our people and he himself built a synagogue for us." . . . Everyone waits for Jesus' response. . . . Jesus nods and follows the elder into Capernaum. . . .

The walk is slow since everyone is following along. . . . Notice just ahead—there is another man rushing toward you. . . . "The Roman officer said not to trouble yourself, Jesus," the man calls out as he makes his way toward Jesus. "He doesn't consider himself worthy to have you enter his house. He says for you to just give the order and his servant will get well. He understands authority and he believes in your authority to perform miracles."

The man waits . . . Jesus just stands looking at the messenger. . . . Jesus' expression changes . . . first to surprise, and then to love. . . . He turns . . . looks at all of you and says, "I tell you, I have never found faith like this, not even in Israel." . . .

Stay with Jesus. . . . Silently experience this moment. . . . Allow Jesus' eyes to look into yours. . . . Do not speak . . . just listen . . . and learn. . . .

Is this the kind of faith Jesus is calling us to have?
. . . What is this experience telling you? . . . What is
Jesus telling you?

Prayer

Jesus, I don't understand how that Roman
officer could have so much faith and trust in your
word. All I know is that he has blindly accepted
God's gift of faith. Jesus, I believe, help my unbelief.
Amen. (Invite spontaneous prayer.)

It is time to leave Jesus. Say good-bye. Turn,
and slowly walk away. Open your eyes and come
back into the room.

Journal Writing

Write down any thoughts, feelings, or
questions that you had during this meditation.

Sharing

After the class has shared their experience and
feelings in small groups and then in the large group,
present the following questions to the group:

■ Why do you suppose Jesus was so surprised at
the Roman officer's faith?

■ Does this surprise mean that the kind of faith Jesus is calling us to is rare?

■ Or, is God's Spirit within us giving us the strength and courage to accept this gift?

■ Can we earn faith?

Journey of Faith

Jesus on the Cross
Matthew 27:45–55;
Mark 15:33–40; Luke 23:44–48;
John 19:17–29

Meditation

The next stop on our faith journey is at a place called Golgotha . . . a place outside of Jerusalem where criminals are executed. This may not be an easy place to be, but it is important to stop here . . . to experience the ultimate of God's love for us and Jesus' blind faith in God's love for him. . . . Close your eyes. . . . Take a deep breath . . . and relax.

You are standing at the foot of a barren rocky hill. . . . The hill is called *Golgotha*. . . . Start climbing up the hill. . . . Feel the unevenness of the ground underneath your feet. . . . Listen! . . . There seems to be much confusion just ahead of you at the top of the hill. . . . Stop. . . . Look up to where all the commotion is—by the three crosses. . . . People are centering their attention on one of those three crosses. . . . It's that center cross. . . . How can these people be poking fun at someone in his last hours of life? . . . Why can't they leave the victims in peace. . . . Wait! . . . Walk closer. . . . That man who is hanging on the center cross . . . the center of ridicule—it's Jesus! . . . Stop a minute to adjust to what you just discovered. . . Jesus . . . hanging on that cross! . . . Near the cross are Roman soldiers tossing dice for Jesus' cloak . . . the very same cloak Mary wove for Jesus . . . the cloak he wore during his public life. . . . Feel the pain and anger within you. . . . Notice that there are a group of women and one man standing silently by the cross. . . . The man has his arms around one woman . . . Jesus' mother. . . . Contemplate her face. . . . Have you ever seen such deep sorrow? . . . Walk up to Mary. . . . Stand with her at the foot of the cross. . . .

Look up now onto the face of Jesus. . . . See the pain and suffering there. . . . Yes, it might be gruesome to look at . . . a gentle face disfigured by blood and dust and pain . . . but it is the face of someone who loves you . . . who has opened up the Kingdom of God for you. . . . Do you believe this? . . . He said so. . . . Or, does the failure and disgrace of Jesus as he hangs here force you to doubt his word? . . . Allow Jesus to look into your eyes . . . to speak to your heart from his cross of shame. . . . I will give you a time of silence for this.

Prayer

Jesus, I do believe in what you taught while walking this earth. It is painful to realize just what you have done for me, for all of us. Lord Jesus, I believe. Help me to follow your teachings, to be open to your gift of faith, to believe that you love me enough to die for me! Amen. (Allow spontaneous prayer also.)

It is time to leave. Turn and slowly walk down the hill. Open your eyes and come back into the room.

Journal Writing

What were your thoughts and feelings while on Golgotha? Write these down and any other thoughts or feelings you have.

Sharing

After small and large-group sharing of feelings, thoughts, and reactions to the meditation, discuss the contradiction of the cross according to the world's standards and what the world calls a successful person and an unsuccessful person. Did it take faith to believe in Jesus' teachings as you stood beneath the cross? Have the teachings of Jesus influenced your life? What does the crucifixion say to you?

Journey of Faith

The Resurrection of Jesus
John 20:24–29

Introduction

This is the final stop on our faith journey. The last place we stopped was at the foot of the cross. There, before the whole world, hung Jesus the failure. We experienced his great love for us. Now it is all important to meet the resurrected Jesus! But first, on our faith journey, we need to be with Thomas the doubter when he meets Jesus.

Meditation

Close your eyes. . . . Take a deep breath . . . and relax. You are in the upper room with Mary and the apostles. This is the same room where Jesus celebrated his Last Supper the night before he died. . . . It seems barren now, doesn't it? . . . Especially compared to the time of the great celebration of the Passover. . . . Notice that the same lanterns still cast dancing shadows on the walls and ceiling, just as they did at the Last Supper. . . . All the women who waited on tables then are now gone . . . but the room is not empty. . . . Look straight ahead. . . . The apostles are here with Mary, Jesus' mother. . . . They seem excited, not at all sad like they have been. . . .

Walk over to Mary and the apostles. . . . Stand next to Peter and Thomas. . . . Look at the contrast of faces. . . . Peter's eyes are bright and he is smiling. Thomas' eyes look sad. He is unsmiling as he keeps shaking his head. . . . Peter is trying to convince Thomas that Jesus is alive and is risen! . . . Peter now turns to Mary. . . . "Mary," he pleads . . . but Thomas puts his hand up and stops him. "Unless I put my finger into the print of the nail in his hand, and unless I put my hand into his side, Peter, I will not believe." . . .

Peter is about to respond. . . . But listen! . . . Someone is saying, "Peace be to you." . . . Look! . . . Over to your left. . . . It is Jesus! . . . He is here, now . . . with you. . . . Alive!

Watch Jesus as he walks over to Thomas, looks into Thomas' eyes, and speaks, . . . "Thomas, put your finger here and look at my hands." Watch Thomas hesitantly place his finger on Jesus' wounds. . . . "Now Thomas," Jesus tells him, . . . "reach out your hand and put it into my side." . . . Thomas places his hand on Jesus' side. . . . Look, he's falling to his knees! . . . Notice that everyone in the room seems to be holding their breath as they watch Thomas. . . . "My Lord and my God!" he exclaims. . . . Watch closely. . . . See the change in

Thomas' face! . . . His eyes are dancing with excitement and love. . . . Jesus now reaches out and raises Thomas to his feet and tells him, "Stop your doubting and believe, Thomas." . . . Thomas and Jesus stand facing each other. . . . Jesus places his hand on Thomas' shoulder and says, "Do you believe because you have seen? . . . Blessed are those who do not see, yet believe." . . .

Spend time now silently just experiencing this moment. What does this say to you?

Prayer

Lord Jesus, so often I am like Thomas. I have to have proof before I believe. Thomas was hurting so much because of your death on the cross that he closed his eyes to what really happened. Jesus, I so often do the very same thing—turn away and close my eyes to your love and guidance in my life. Lord, I believe, help my unbelief. Amen. (Invite spontaneous prayer.)

It is time to leave this upper room in the city of Jerusalem. Turn and begin to walk away. Open your eyes, and come back into this room.

Journal Writing

Write down the thoughts and feelings you had during this meditation. Do not discount any thought you had.

Sharing

Share thoughts and feelings the class had during the meditation, first in small groups and then in a large group. For further discussion, the class can share their experiences of doubt about God and the power of God in their lives.

You can also have a debate. One side understands Thomas' disbelief; the other side questions Thomas' disbelief. Have someone write student comments on the board.

Journey of Faith Follow-Up

1. Give the class time to read over their journals, write any further thoughts they might have, and also write their thoughts and reactions to the journey of faith.

2. Divide into small groups, no more than five or so in a group, and have each group choose a group recorder. Give the groups time to share their thoughts, feelings, and general reactions to their faith journey. Suggested questions they can discuss are as follows:

■ Has the blind faith of those we met in these meditations affected your life today? If so, how? If not, why not?

■ Do you think it is possible for you today to experience a situation that calls you to walk in blind faith? If so, give examples. If not, why not?

■ Which meditation influenced you the most? Give reasons for your choice.

■ What conclusion(s) have you come to from this faith journey?

3. Have the students come together. The recorder of each group shares the thoughts of their group. Allow for a general discussion.

Class Experiment

1. Class returns to small groups. Each group has a blindfold. Each one in the group takes a turn being led blindfolded around the room by a member of their group.

2. Small group stands in a close circle with one member in the center who closes his or her eyes and falls backwards allowing the others to catch him or her.

3. Discuss experience and feelings in the large group.

Closing Liturgy

Preparation: The class is given time to express their faith creatively:

■ by creating a class mural on which they can draw or paste pictures expressing their faith.

■ by writing a poem or psalm and placing it on the mural.

■ by writing statements of faith.

■ by putting music to a poem someone has written, or by putting a poem to a song they know.

Give the class time to do these things, especially for *each* student to write a statement of faith.

Liturgy

Have prepared a table on which is placed a candle, the cross, and any other decorations the class wishes. Suggested music would be *Hosea.*

Have the students gather around the altar table with their creations of faith. Give them time to share these creations.

As the music is heard in the background, each student quietly places her or his statement of faith on the Bible. Invite anyone who wishes to share their statement of faith to do so before placing it on the Bible.

In closing, the young people join hands in a circle around the Bible and sing, *Here I Am, Lord.*

Suggested Music: *Follow Me* by Ray Repp (K and R Music); *Hosea* (Weston Priory); *Come and Journey with Me* by David Haas (GIA Publications); *Let Your Light Shine* by Ron Griffen (Leaven Productions).